The First Date Dress

LAURA GIROIR SMESTAD

DEDICATION

To the friends who listened to my dating stories without complaint, to the men who showed me how it felt to be treated with respect, and to the women who are still struggling to find their self-worth.

PREFACE

My name is Laura, and there is nothing special about me. I am not beautiful, interesting, or worthy of real love.

What bullshit.

Sadly, that was the view I had of myself when my marriage of six years dissolved, leaving me fragmented and unsure as I attempted to build a new life on my own. But that is only a piece of what this book covers. Mostly, it's about dating in the digital age, a phenomenon I did not experience until I was a 28-year-old divorcée forced to find myself (and potentially my future partner) in a technologically-driven time. I dove without caution into a resolutely ambivalent world in which it's perfectly normal to procure dates with the swipe of my finger, and I accumulated enough noteworthy stories to warrant writing this book. I am under no illusion that I am the only woman to experience uncomfortable dates, unexpected ghosting, unwanted hickeys, and distasteful Tinder openers*, but I have noticed that we are lacking

---

* My favorite opening line I've received being, "What does your butthole taste like?"

a female voice willing to commit to paper the maddening and often humorous struggles many of us face when dating in today's world. So, yes, this book details my most outlandish stories from a year of dating men found through Bumble, Tinder, Hinge, OkCupid, Coffee Meets Bagel, and, occasionally, real life; but it also recounts my journey towards self-discovery, self-growth, and, eventually, self-love. Of course, all names in this book (except for my own) have been altered. My hope is that throughout your reading adventure you find my accounts to be amusing and relatable while recognizing the underlying theme that you are enough as you are and that your worth is NEVER determined by a romantic partner**.

** Even if he is kind enough to inquire about your booty-hole's flavor when messaging you on Tinder

THE FIRST DATE DRESS

TABLE OF CONTENTS

CHAPTER ONE

The First Date Dress

My OLIVE-GREEN T-SHIRT DRESS is the ultimate first date dress. It's short enough to show off my legs and conservative enough on top to not give everything away. It's the perfect combination of cute and sexy while maintaining a slight air of mystery. It can be dressed up with heels and jewelry for a date at a fancy cocktail bar or dressed down with sandals and a sweater for a casual coffee date. I feel like a confident badass in this dress.

Fun fact about me: I am a stubborn, determined, all-in woman. I don't know how to live among irresolute "should haves" or tentative "what ifs," and I often find myself incapable of yielding to any moment in which I do not offer 120% of myself. That being said, it will come as no surprise that when I was tossed into the world of dating for the first time in my adult life, I downloaded every dating app imaginable with reckless abandon in hopes of finding my perfect mate. What I didn't realize at the time is that it was actually myself I was so intent on finding.

Nevertheless, I dated. I dated lawyers, musicians, engineers, analysts, interior decorators, chefs, financial advisors, and military officers. I dated men with short hair, long hair, brown hair, blonde hair, red hair, and no hair. I dated guys who were passionate about science, video games, football, literature, movies, running, conspiracy theories, and themselves. I dated in the evenings after work, on weekend afternoons, and every Saturday night. And through all of this dating, I was searching. I was scanning the city for a man who fit my list of an ideal partner because, in my mind, taking charge of this pursuit meant I was strong enough to never settle for less again.

What I failed to recognize was that the unfruitful search for my elusive "forever person" actually neglected pieces of myself that needed time to bloom, ironically mirroring the neglect I experienced in past relationships. I should have been looking at *myself* as my "forever person" instead of a man. Of course, if the version of myself who knows that my identity is not and should not be rooted in another person had existed at this point in the story, you would be reading a very different, less entertaining book.

Now let's get back to the first date dress (it is the title of the book after all). In addition to my stubborn nature, I am also extremely logical and efficient, and I concluded early on that I would wear my olive-green dress on every first date. Due to the sheer volume of first dates I found myself agreeing to attend, and because most of these dates didn't result in a second, if I did happen to like someone enough to go out with him again, I wanted to avoid the hassle of locating the memory of what he already saw me wearing. This isn't usually a problem for most people, but those of you who have ever consistently gone on 6 to 10 first dates in a week know it's easy to lose track of wardrobe choices. I can only imagine what the baristas at my favorite coffee shop and the bartenders at my go-to bar (both of which I often suggested as first date options) thought as they saw me coming in with different guys night after night wearing the same green dress.

While the first date dress was mostly about practicality—ensuring my date never inferred that I only owned one article of clothing—it was also about beginning to manufacture confidence. As you can probably tell from the opening lines of this book, my self-worth was abysmally low when I began this journey. Finding a dress that I knew looked great on me, paired with precisely applied makeup and meticulously curled hair provided me with high levels of false confidence.

I distinctly remember saying things like, "If someone doesn't like me for exactly who I am, that's not the person I want to date," while in the next breath asking my friend for an opinion on how I should present myself that same night.

I found myself obsessing over whether or not my date thought I was beautiful and interesting, even if I didn't like him. Let me repeat that. *I spent time agonizing over the opinion of a man who I literally did not even want to date.* Why? Because I didn't yet believe that I actually possessed those qualities. And no matter how many men told me I was gorgeous or funny or smart or vibrant, that couldn't change how I felt about myself. Only I had the power to do that*.

As you can imagine, this period of intense dating was short-lived, mostly because it was exhausting. At the time, I was working full-time as a mental health counselor in a school

---

* For those of you still struggling with making this realization, it took me a long time to see my own power and worth because as women we are conditioned to see the opposite.

helping over 500 tiny humans and their parents, which was also tiring by nature (I am convinced that children have as much energy as they do because they suck it from the adults around them). I was also teaching group fitness classes on the weekends and working on my Ph.D. while fitting in time for family and friends on top of my new-found hobby of serial dating. Looking back at my calendar, I honestly don't know how I sustained that lifestyle for as long as I did.

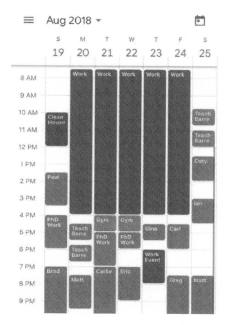

You'll see in the following chapters that the quality of men who made it into this book gradually improve as I move along in my discovery of who I am and what I want, and I think that my decision to slow down the race to find my person accounts for a large percentage of that uptick. I believe that the rest of that change resides in the personal self-work I did, which gave me substantial insight into what kind of person I want to date.

You've probably inferred by now that I am a *little* type A, so, of course, I actually wrote out a list to catalogue my ideal partner's characteristics. Eventually, I came to see that this list was not as important as I originally thought it would be. In fact, I pieced together that the only three guys who I deemed to be men who "checked all of my boxes" were the only three guys who flat out rejected me. I was so excited about these men that I recall gushing about them to my friends because they actually met my criteria. It was almost as if I was reciting their resumes instead of talking about who they actually were as people. Gainfully employed...check! Master's degree from a prestigious university...check! Dependable and punctual...check!**

The interesting thing is that each one of these guys claimed "lack of spark" as the rationale for not wanting to continue past a second date, and I wonder if my intent focus on checkboxes and lists made me gravitate towards men with whom I didn't have any real chemistry. Looking back, I think I convinced myself there was a spark in those instances purely because I couldn't pass up someone who fit my cookie-cutter ideal of a future partner.

** I'm eye rolling so hard at my past self as I write this.

After this realization, I trimmed my list down to the most important pieces. Doing this allowed me to let go of things that weren't truly important (like level of education) and to prioritize the things I know I need in a relationship (like solid communication). Even with this streamlined list, it was only when I completely resigned the idea of finding my ideal "forever person" that I finally experienced what it was like to be treated the way I deserved. Because at that point, I was already my own "forever person."

None of the men in this book are terrible people. There are a few who I honestly didn't get a chance to know very well either because we only went on a few dates or because they weren't willing to be emotionally open at the time. I also want to add the disclaimer that not all of the dates I went on were bad, and I had plenty of great conversations with interesting men who just weren't the right fit for me romantically. And as for the lesser quality dates? Now you get to read about some of them.

THE FIRST DATE DRESS

CHAPTER TWO

Corsage Guy

IT ALL BEGINS with Corsage Guy. We matched on Bumble in August of 2018, just before I left on a road trip with my best friend. One night of the trip, when my friend went to sleep early, Corsage Guy asked if we could talk on the phone because he didn't want to wait until we met in person to hear my voice. I swooned over that sentiment because I hate texting and would always prefer to talk to

THE FIRST DATE DRESS

somebody in person or on the phone (a dying, underrated form of communication in my opinion). We ended up talking for three hours that evening, during which two interesting facts emerged: 1. He once took a class to learn how to perfect his oral sex skills and 2. At the tender age of 18, he worked as a stripper and apparently still had the dance moves to prove it.

Some of you may be excited by this information and are thinking, "Yes, girl! Go get your own personal Magic Mike." I, however, thought it was a little strange that he led with that material prior to our meeting. On one hand, I appreciated his honesty. On the other, it seemed like he was bragging about those things to get me to like him more, which left me with a weird feeling. I now know this weird feeling to be my intuition, and this is the first example of many when I chose to ignore it.

After our first phone conversation, things started moving at an impractically quick pace. We hadn't even met, and he was already calling me every day and consistently sending snapchat videos of him serenading me with boyband songs in his car to let me know he was thinking of me*. I'm not going to lie, the attention felt really, really good, so, I went with it. By the time I was back from my trip and we were about to embark on our first date, he had already expressed that he saw something special between us and promised he would never hurt me.

I may have ignored a few red flags because I was infatuated with the prospect of my first Bumble match turning out to be my "forever person." It would have been such an adorable story if the whole thing wasn't so contrived.

---

* That's a typical casual dating move, right?

Let me pause the story to describe what I call the "too much, too soon guy" and why I stopped dating that archetype. The "too much, too soon guy," as you can probably guess, does way too much way too soon. It's as if the beginning stages of dating are completely skipped and you jump to the part where he's sending you good morning messages and talks about your future dog (or weirder, future children). It feels great at first because surely that level of attentiveness is a sign that this guy is incredibly into you and really sees a future together. But, as many of you know, intensity at the very beginning typically isn't sustainable. In my experience with "too much, too soon guys," once I finally started reciprocating in similar ways because I was beginning to invest, they backed off, which used to leave me feeling as if there was something wrong with me and how I show affection. My own theory, which has been confirmed by a few of my male friends, is that "too much, too soon guys" pull out all the stops at the beginning to court a partner, and at some point, when they feel secure enough they won't lose that person, they relax and revert to however it is they would usually act.

I know that we all tend to present the best version of ourselves early on in dating, but acting as the very best you enhanced by a million can be misleading (and I'm sure exhausting for the person doing too much). While it seems counterintuitive, I've found that the healthiest dating situations I've experienced have been ones that started slow. Maybe we went a few days without talking or a few weeks without seeing each other. Maybe we didn't try to cram our whole life stories into the first three dates. Maybe we slowly built a friendship base, and things progressed from there. Initially, that slow-moving garnering of attention could be misinterpreted as lack of interest, but really it allows things to develop at a more natural pace.

Corsage Guy was definitely a "too much, too soon guy." After the exchange of numerous phone calls, snaps, and text messages, I finally returned from my trip, and we scheduled our first date. He decided to take me to a fancy restaurant for dinner, and I was beyond excited. In fact, I tried on five different dresses, sending photos of all of the options to my friends for approval**. I even put on perfume, which I very rarely do. In my mind, that night was going to be magical.

Now, in hindsight, I made two mistakes in scheduling that date. First, I agreed to let him pick me up from my house. I suppose some people may not have a huge issue with this, but everyone I've told has reacted as if I invited a serial killer into my home, which, I guess for all I knew, could have been the case. I haven't made

---

** None of which were what was soon to become the official first date dress...

that safety error again. Second, I agreed to dinner on the first date. I know people have differing opinions on this one, but I think we all can agree that dinner is a lot more difficult to slip away from if things go south, especially if your date is also your means of transportation. After this, I stuck to meeting guys for coffee or drinks on date #1 to avoid potential future pitfalls.

But in this story, I let Corsage Guy pick me up and take me to dinner. He came to my door, dressed in a nice suit, and told me I looked stunning as he walked into my living room. His hands were behind his back as he took a glance around the room, which I thought was strange. Was he just nervous? Did he bring me chocolate? Did he have a knife and was preparing to murder me? The truth was not something I anticipated, although maybe something I should have suspected when he

THE FIRST DATE DRESS

called me earlier in the day to ask what color dress I was wearing to dinner; the question reminded me of boys in high school asking about the color of my dress before a school dance. I'll never forget the image of him—with a proud smile on his face—as he procured from behind his back a clear plastic box containing a wrist corsage.

Yes, you read that right. HE BROUGHT ME A CORSAGE.

I thought it was a joke, so I just laughed a little, said thank you, and put the box on my coffee table before I grabbed my purse. He did not laugh. Instead, he asked incredulously, "You aren't going to wear it?" I said no. Instead of accepting this, he asked why I didn't want to wear it, so I told him it was because I look like

I'm 16 years old,*** and he was going to risk looking like a pedophile taking me to a homecoming dance. He looked hurt, so as a compromise, I wore it in his truck on the way to the restaurant.

I honestly don't remember many details from dinner, aside from the fact that the crab cake appetizer we shared was exceptionally delicious, but I do remember Corsage Guy telling me that I possessed all of the qualities necessary to be a good military wife (I should probably mention that he is in the military, otherwise that statement would sound even weirder than it already does). I should have been a little concerned that on the first date he was already talking about how I would hypothetically fit into his lifestyle if things ever headed towards marriage, but for some unknown reason, I brushed off another red flag.

*** In addition to being 5'1, I had braces at the time.

Actually, that's not the truth. I know exactly why I ignored the strange behavior, and it has nothing to do with my self-esteem issues or even simply wanting male attention. Corsage Guy was gorgeous. Absolutely, he-might-actually-be-photoshopped gorgeous, and I have no doubts in my mind that he made ridiculous amounts of money in his days as an exotic dancer. That factor, along with my tendency at the time to give an abundance of chances before cutting things off, meant that I went out with him again despite the corsage and odd level of intensity. Luckily for you, that means the story isn't over yet.

Between our first and second dates, Corsage Guy did a romantic thing. Or at least it would have been romantic if we had spent more than only a few hours together. He told me that he booked a beach vacation for us to go away for Labor Day weekend, AND he sent me his

Airbnb receipt showing he had paid over $700 for the beach condo rental. *WTF.* Even past Laura knew that was strange, but I didn't say anything at first in order to give things a fair chance. I thought, "Who knows? Maybe by Labor Day he'll be my boyfriend, and I'll regret saying no now."

Our schedules didn't align until the following week, so in the interim between dates, we returned to our daily texts and nightly phone calls. For our second date, we decided to cook dinner together at my place, meaning we skipped right into relationship mode. Yes, a bit much for a second date, but I guess that's the theme of this chapter. This time when he came over, he brought ingredients to make chicken curry instead of a corsage, and we cooked dinner while sharing moments from our days. He even did the dishes.

I thought that maybe things would work out with the gorgeous man who did strange things. However, even with this hope, I did express concern about the proposed beach trip. Specifically, I asked how he would feel if I went on the trip and wasn't ready to sleep with him at that point. Corsage Guy assured me that he would never pressure me to do anything I wasn't ready for, and he even offered to sleep on the floor if that made me more comfortable. A little extreme, especially given that he spent a ridiculous amount of money on the condo, but okay.

Immediately following this conversation, he pulled me toward him and started kissing me with such ferocity that I started to feel uncomfortable. Something felt off, but I ignored my internal alarm despite my discomfort. The dichotomy of Corsage Guy saying he would sleep on the floor to ensure he doesn't cross any boundaries and then suddenly becoming almost aggressively physical made me feel uneasy.

From what I recall, I think I eventually made up some excuse of being tired instead of asking him to slow down because I didn't want to hurt his feelings, and I still don't understand why I placed his feelings above my own in that moment.

The next day, I texted him to say I couldn't go on the beach trip. Then, he ghosted. The guy who so intensely pursued me even weeks before we met in person and who said he didn't want to fall asleep without hearing my voice on the phone simply didn't respond.

Remember how I said I put too much

emphasis on what a guy thought of me even if I didn't want to date him? Well, this was the perfect example. I didn't really want to see him again, although I probably would have if he had asked because I was still in my 'ignore red flags' stage, but, even so, I was angry that he disappeared. If you're thinking there's absolutely no logic in that whatsoever, you would be correct. I'm sure my friends remember me being irrationally upset over this guy, and I can almost guarantee they were wondering why I would care at all that the guy who gave me a weird wrist flower on our first date didn't respond to my text. I did a crazy person thing a few days later and texted Corsage Guy to tell him he was a shitty person for ghosting, especially since he promised he was "different" from other guys. At the time, I was disappointed and offended. Writing this over a year later, I can't help but laugh at how stupid it was to let any guy— ESPECIALLY CORSAGE GUY—have such an effect on my emotions.

Because, in reality, the behavior of others usually has nothing to do with us. So why do so many people internalize others' actions? I think it's part egocentricity and part a need for external validation. Either way, when I learned to stop tying my happiness and self-worth to how men acted toward me, I was able to see myself more clearly and enter into a much healthier state of mind. Who knows why Corsage Guy ghosted? At the time, I was sure that it was because I wasn't enough in some way, but realistically, he probably met someone else or had a bruised ego after I said no to the trip or was dealing with his own personal struggles. The reason doesn't matter because even if his reason for ghosting was that he didn't like some aspect of me, that does not dictate my worth as a woman.

I've heard many people express the desire to find their "other half," and I've heard partners say to each other, "You complete me." I think both of those sayings are ridiculous. They imply that we are not whole beings by ourselves but rather only when joined with another person. I would rather view it as 'I am a whole person, you are a whole person, and together we are two kickass humans who come together to be even more awesome than we are alone.' In my ideal relationship, we enhance each other's lives instead of filling an incomplete part of the other person.

Whatever you believe about romantic partners "completing" each other, I think it's pretty clear that Corsage Guy was never going to be that person for me. The story, however, doesn't end with his ghosting maneuver. A month later, Corsage Guy sent me a Facebook message that simply said, "Sorry." I was going to respond by telling him it was okay—because by that time I had come to my senses enough to see his departure as a positive thing—but he must have blocked me after his message because I couldn't reply. Such heartbreak. At least in the end I got an entertaining story, a weak apology, and the ugliest corsage I've ever seen in my life.

THE FIRST DATE DRESS

CHAPTER THREE

Neck Guy

My SECOND DATING app experience, which was my first foray into Tinder, started with a seemingly abundant supply of potential. As you'll soon see, the ending left something to be desired. Let me introduce you to Neck Guy. Neck Guy seemed so great that, until date four, you'll have a difficult time understanding why he made it into the early chapters of this book.

Neck Guy and I already had plans in place for our first date when I found myself looking for something to do on a Saturday night, but I took a chance and asked if he wanted to meet up sooner than intended to grab a drink with me that evening. He was out with his friends at a major event in the city (one that I was actually supposed to attend with my friend), and he invited me to join. I thanked him for the offer but politely declined, mostly because I didn't want to deal with fighting traffic and battling for parking downtown on what I knew would be a crowded night.

I figured I would spend my time reading in my pajamas with a glass of wine before retiring to bed early, but instead, he offered to send an Uber for me to meet him and his friends at the event. This gesture at least seemed more appropriate than a corsage, so I quickly agreed to the plan. We had a wonderful night. I liked him, I liked his friends, and our evening didn't end until he kindly offered to Uber me home from a dance club at 1 am.

I couldn't wait to see him again, and—right on cue—Neck Guy texted me the following morning with an offer to hang out by his pool. When the text arrived, I was attempting to assemble my living room furniture (which had arrived in about 100,000 pieces with no instructions), and his second date proposal fluttered across my phone just as I contemplated thrusting a screwdriver into my eye. My frustration with that process, coupled with the fantasy of relaxing by a pool with a handsome man, blinded me from seeing the "too much, too soon guy" red flag that accompanied this two-dates-in-two-days invitation.

As we sipped drinks by his pool, I expressed my annoyance with my own superb lack of handiness, and he immediately offered to come over the next evening to help put together my tables and tv stand. As much as I was determined to complete the task on my own as an educated, independent woman, I admitted defeat and accepted his assistance. Now we were looking at three days of consecutive dates. I once again ignored the red flag waving boldly in the depths of my mind, mostly because I was still clueless, and partially because I was desperate to have functioning furniture in my living room.

Honestly, it felt really great to know that this guy was so interested in me that he wanted to see me every day, especially after spending so much of my time in my past relationships feeling unwanted and disregarded. I so badly desired to feel important to someone, anyone, that I was already creating scenarios in my head in which we were in a serious relationship. I guess maybe at the time I was a "too much, too soon" girl.

Most of us happen upon daydreams in the initial stages of dating, thinking about what could be because we're excited by possibilities. However, the problem with allowing our imaginations to steal the show is that we often create a version of the other person in our minds that may not actually exist in reality. I would regularly find myself lost in these types of daydreams, concocting a recipe for the perfect partner, with each new guy playing the starring role in my mental film, picking up right where I left off with the last one. It amazes me to look back at how interchangeable they were.

It's no surprise then that I fell into this pattern with Neck Guy. All I knew about him was that he had a steady job, a solid education, a kind demeanor, and a spectacular smile. That, combined with the fact that he spent hours assembling my furniture, was enough for my imagination to run wild with fragments of who he actually was and form an idea of him that probably never could have existed. There is no perfect person.

But, yes, Neck Guy came over the next evening and spent four and a half hours putting together my furniture. We played music and laughed while he occasionally struggled to figure out the next steps, and I once again thought that maybe he could be that person for whom I was searching. Aligning with the theme of too-much-too-soon, I offered to cook dinner for him as a thank you for his labor*.

---

* At least this time I waited until the 4th date instead of the 2nd to start staying in and cooking?

After a one-day break from seeing each other, I arrived at his apartment, grocery bags in hand, ready to show off my culinary skills. When I arrived, however, his friend was over at his apartment playing video games. I thought that was a little strange, considering that was the time he had invited me to come over. He asked if I wouldn't mind if he and his friend finished one level of the game they had been trying to beat, and I—trying to be the ultimate cool chick—said that I had no problem whatsoever with the situation. If it really had been just one quick round of a game, maybe it wouldn't have bothered me, but I spent almost an hour watching Neck Guy and his bestie repeatedly die in a Mario game.

I watched and watched and the whole time pretended to be manic-pixie-dream-girl-cool about it, the supporting actress to his boyish Peter Pan type behaviors. Eventually, his friend's girlfriend was "nagging him" to come home, so he begrudgingly left us to our date.

I started cooking, and Neck Guy occasionally asked to be assigned small tasks to help, like chopping an onion. The scenario was really sweet until I no longer had a job for him to complete, and instead of hanging out with me as I cooked, he declared that he was retreating to the living room to play Mario. That's right, readers: on our fourth date, I cooked for Neck Guy, and halfway through, he left me with pots and pans as my sole company while he fought to defeat Bowser #priorities.

While I waited for water to boil, I sat next to him on the couch, convinced that he would suddenly pay attention to me because of sheer proximity. I was wrong. He continued to play and ignore me so profusely that I momentarily questioned whether or not I had accidentally acquired the power of invisibility. As I awkwardly sat beside him, I looked through Instagram stories with a naïve hope that he would put the game controller down and at least ask me an inane question like whether or not I have any siblings. Obviously, that never happened, so instead, I ventured back to the kitchen to finish cooking.

After eating dinner, we decided to watch a movie. Keeping with the theme of a disappointing evening, he fell asleep on me within the first 30 minutes. Like literally *on* me. And that, friends, is how I ended up watching *Monsters, Inc.* by myself on my fourth Tinder date with Neck Guy, the weight of his body crushing my shoulder *and* my fantasy of him.

If I found myself in that situation recently, I

would have done a few things differently. First of all, I wouldn't have offered to cook for a guy on the fourth date. But if that were still the scenario, I would have certainly asked if he and his friend could play their game another time because I was there to spend time with him, not his Wii. If he later vocalized a desire to abandon me to play Mario, I would have asked him if we could talk instead. And finally, if he fell asleep on me during a movie after all of that, I would have woken him up instead of solo-watching a Pixar film with his snoring as an additional soundtrack. Basically, I would have set appropriate boundaries.

Some of you may be wondering why I didn't. In short, I wanted him to like me. I was so afraid that if I didn't simply roll with these annoyances, he wouldn't want to see me anymore, which is funny considering I wasn't even sure I wanted to continue seeing *him*.

I was also accepting what I thought I deserved at the time. He was cute and smart and liked me, so how could I expect that he would respect me as well? In my mind, that was asking for too much. I couldn't comprehend at the time that there could be someone out there who would treat me well and who would *want* to treat me well.

Someone who would appreciate me exactly as I am.

Someone who would choose me over a video game.

Someone who would choose *me*.

I did a lot of settling out of fear that if I did happen to stumble across a man who encompassed all of the qualities that were important to me in a partner, maybe he wouldn't

41

THE FIRST DATE DRESS

want me. Why would I believe he would? My past relationships taught me that I was not important, that I had to change myself in order to be loved, and that I would never matter to a man in the same way he mattered to me. I am so sad for the version of myself who blindly trusted these ideas without question. I wish I could wrap her in my arms and tell her that she deserves to be given love out of the same depths from which she gives and that she will find someone amazing who accepts her fiercely and completely. Though, I don't know if she would be ready to hear it.

After Neck Guy awoke from his slumber, I kissed him goodnight and drove home. Before I even made it back to my house, Neck Guy sent the following text:

Hey...sorry again for falling asleep on you. At least I wasn't tindering while we were together though. It looked like you were swiping pretty hard at one point...

I couldn't believe that after his impressive lack of consideration all evening he would have the audacity to accuse me of looking for my next Tinder match while sitting next to him. If he had looked over at me even once during that time, he would have easily seen that I was swiping through Instagram stories, but clearly, he couldn't be bothered to do so. I expressed that I was offended by his statement and that I was not in fact on Tinder during any part of our date.

He apologized.

I agreed to another date.

This time, we had four whole days apart before we saw each other at a pool party he was hosting. My feelings of disappointment from our last date had begun to thaw after the time apart, and I decided to let it go and enjoy my time with him and his friends. The party was fun but mostly uneventful, and after his guests departed, we went up to his apartment. He put on another movie and actually stayed awake this time, although, in the aftermath, I certainly wished he had fallen asleep again.

About halfway through the movie, we started making out. Everything was fine until he started biting my lip—not in a sexy nibble kind of way, but in a he-might-puncture-my-lip kind of way. I pulled back a little (when I actually should have just vocalized that I wasn't a fan of the lip biting), and he started kissing my neck instead. That was better than the lip thing, so I let him continue. When he took my shirt off, I told him that I wasn't going to sleep with him that night just to ensure there would be no miscommunications, and he assured me that wasn't a problem. Apparently, he did think it was a problem though, because as we were making out, he took off his pants and tried to have sex with me anyway. I stopped him and told him again that I wasn't ready to sleep with him yet, and at least that time he accepted my declaration. We continued to have a mediocre make out/fool around session**, and afterwards, I left.

When I got home, I stood in front of my mirror, and I could not believe my eyes. Or rather, I could not believe my neck and the number of hickeys covering it. I looked like a murder victim on *Forensic Files* who had been strangled to death.

** During which he so kindly asked, "Hey, wanna go to my bed and 69?"

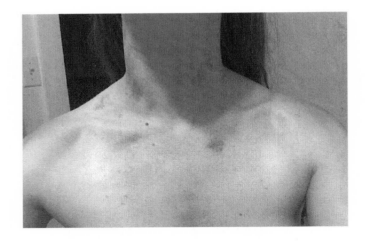

I sent him a picture of the damage, and he asked for forgiveness.

I didn't respond for five days.

To make the situation even more pleasurable, the hickeys were significantly more pronounced the following morning, just in time for me to present to the *entire faculty at my school.* Oh, and did I mention that this story takes place in *August in the south?* Needless to say, a turtleneck sweater would have seemed questionable in the 100-degree heat.

Thankfully, I own a sleeveless turtleneck dress, so I wore that for my presentation and no one was the wiser (my friends who knew about my neck situation assured me it was well concealed). The hickeys took almost a full week to disappear enough for me to adequately cover them with concealer alone, so the rest of the week, I took to wearing colorful, light, summer scarves. Some of the older ladies at school gave me very sweet compliments about these scarves, and I wanted so badly to respond by saying "Thanks, they're fashionable but also completely necessary."

I still hadn't responded to Neck Guy, but I also don't believe in ghosting, so I sent him a text apologizing for going MIA and telling him I didn't think it was going to work out. He said he was sorry again for the hickeys and assured me they were not intentional. Right. I haven't had a hickey since I was 16 (and even my high school boyfriend *knew* he was leaving a mark), but a 29-year-old "man" can brand me for a full week without noticing the damage he was inflicting.

I told Neck Guy that I wasn't holding a grudge but that I didn't want to move forward.

He asked me to dinner.

I never responded.

CHAPTER FOUR

Game of Thrones Guy

Have you ever looked back on a time you dated someone and thought that it was mostly just a waste of time, but you didn't end things sooner because nothing was really *wrong*, everything just wasn't quite right? For me, that was Game of Thrones Guy (GoTG). I hesitated to write this chapter at first because it isn't nearly as exciting as the others, but in the end, I thought it was only fair to represent the very real experience so many women have of finding themselves in lackluster dating situations, sticking around because it isn't particularly bad or good.

I matched with GoTG on Tinder less than a month after my hickeys faded. Eager to shut down my exhausting serial dating operation, I was excited to find a guy who I wanted to see for more than just one evening and who overall seemed like a decent person. Mirroring most of our time together, our first date was unremarkable. I had a good time (but not a great time); we had a good connection (but not a great connection); we drank good wine (but not great wine). The entire month or so we dated, I was exceptionally ambivalent.

Despite the exceedingly average experience, I did learn a few important lessons from GoTG, mostly regarding sex. First lesson: Consent is nonnegotiable. Second lesson: I cannot be sexually attracted to someone who I think is stupid (that will come into play a bit later).

Let's start with lesson one, because, let's face it, some of you are wondering when I'm finally going to get laid in this book*.

At the end of our second date, GoTG and I went back to my place to watch a movie. When the credits rolled, we began to make out, and I once again found myself telling a guy that I didn't want to have sex too soon into dating him. He said he was fine with it—and rightfully so since he still got a pretty killer blow job out of the deal.

---

* In case you're curious, I'm not a prude, and I do enjoy sex. I just tend to hold out for a little while before sleeping with someone to make sure he actually likes me instead of only wanting to fuck me.

After our third date, we found ourselves at my house again, and when we started kissing that time, he asked if I wanted to go to my bedroom. I told him I thought that might lead to something I wasn't quite ready for yet, and he assured me that we didn't have to do anything we haven't already done. Of course, I believed him, and I followed him to my room.

As we continued our makeout session in my bed, clothes came off, piece by piece, and GoTG started going down on me[**]. After a while, he came back up to kiss me, and then—much to my surprise—I felt him push inside of me. It didn't even occur to me at the time that I could or should try to stop him. After all, it was already happening. And this, my friends, is where things started to get muddled in my mind. Since the sex turned out to be good, I

[**] Surprisingly the only part of my experience with him that was definitively above average

managed to convince myself it was okay that he deliberately ignored my statement that I wasn't ready for it, especially because there was a decent chance I would have said yes at that point if he had asked me anyway. In my mind, because I was turned on and had a good time, it was fine that I never actually consented.

For the record, THAT IS NOT THE CORRECT RESPONSE, LADIES.

It did bother me deep in my gut, especially since he didn't even use a condom, but my rationale for continuing to see him was that I had already slept with him, and therefore, since he was added to my body count, I should just continue to sleep with him. That completely illogical thought—coupled with my unfortunate habit at the time of feeling attached to someone after the first instances of physical intimacy—

means that I carried on with our dating situation and never brought it up to him.

Despite this less than desirable start, there were glimmers of promise with GoTG. We spent a lot of time together, mostly watching *Game of Thrones* through his HBO account (believe it or not, I still hadn't seen the series), and he would make me stovetop popcorn from a special pot that his grandmother left him when she died. He kept the popcorn pot at my house to ease my anxiety around the idea that he was going to suddenly want to stop seeing me.

We would go to dinner, watch TV, have lots of sex, and then talk for hours. It was the first time that I felt as if a guy genuinely wanted to listen to me. One night, after I expressed that I had a particularly difficult day, GoTG showed up at my place with ice cream and attentively listened as I talked about a wave of grief that swept over me when I received paperwork for my annulment that afternoon, which contained a fun questionnaire for me to complete with intimate details about my failed marriage.

Once my deluge of feelings subsided, he held me, and I told him how much I appreciated him taking the time to listen to me on a day I was struggling because I had never experienced that before with a romantic partner. His initial response was, "Wow, that's sad."

And it was sad. Prior to my life as a serial dater, I was a serial monogamist, and from the time I was 13 until my divorce at 28, I was consistently in long term relationship after long term relationship. That means in 15 years—including an 8-year-long relationship (6 of those years married)—I couldn't summon a single memory of a man holding me and intently listening to me express my feelings without being dismissive, trying to solve the problem, or withdrawing at the first sign of emotion.

That's where the bar was set for GoTG: Be a decent human to me, and I will be yours despite all of the ways we aren't right for each other.

There were a lot of ways we weren't right for each other.

There were two things in particular on my "ideal partner" list that I decided to momentarily forget about because GoTG so clearly did not fit them.

1. My ideal partner is driven and has goals in life.

2. My ideal partner is not dependent on any substances for happiness.

A big problem with GoTG for me (and I recognize that this is not even remotely a deal-breaker for a lot of people), was that he didn't really seem to be going anywhere in life or have any concrete goals. When I met him, GoTG was an office manager and an aspiring musician. A few weeks later, he decided to quit his job and join his family's business so he could focus on his music, primarily wanting to score films one day. I actually thought that long-term goal was pretty cool; however, he made no actual moves to achieve it, so in hindsight, it was more of a dream than a goal.

A few weeks after that, he expressed interest in becoming a firefighter. The desire for this, however, was inspired by the amount of "free time" he would have and the ease of securing the job since a relative was able to put in a good word for him. There was a lot of talk around him pursuing that, but I'm not sure if any action was ever taken (it at least didn't happen while we were still seeing each other).

So, what did GoTG do with his free time if he wasn't busy crushing goals? He was getting high. While it's definitely not the worst thing he could be doing, it bothered me how dependent he seemed on smoking weed. According to him, it made his "music transcend," and it was a "very important part of [his] life." He also spent a lot of time talking about getting high. It appeared to be a focal point in his world, and it was not in mine.

Neither of those things were terrible—they just didn't match a few of my personal preferences. So again, I stuck around because nothing was really bad, even though nothing was really good.

It also didn't seem like things were actually moving forward with us, and when I asked him a little over a month in if he could see things progressing further, he responded that he was "open" to whatever happened. That's a phrase that I eventually learned means, 'I don't want to be in a relationship with you, and even though we're spending almost all of our free time together, going on dates, sharing deep thoughts, not seeing other people, and for all intents and purposes acting like a couple, I'm not looking for anything serious. However, I do want to continue to *hang out* with you and bang you indefinitely even though I know I'm wasting your time because you're looking for a relationship.'

That was the other phrase I learned to pick up on over time—"hanging out" in lieu of "dating." The few guys I went on dates with who were "open" to whatever may come also only referred to what we were doing as "hanging out." Even when we were going to dinner or a movie, it was never referred to as a date, which now I know was because they never had any intentions of *actually* dating me in any meaningful way.

Even though it looked like we were going to remain stagnant, I still wasn't eager to end things because I was so indifferent toward the whole situation. At least he was a decent guy who liked spending time with me. At least he paid attention to me. At least I wasn't alone.

Eventually, my apathy came to a halt when I learned my second lesson about sex from GoTG: I cannot be sexually attracted to someone if I'm not also intellectually attracted.

One day, GoTG and I were hanging out by a pool, and I was talking to him about my family, specifically saying how I wish my mom would talk to a therapist about the struggles she faced in caring for my dad, who was disabled and very ill. GOTG explained that he didn't understand the point in therapy. "How would talking to someone about your problems help anything?"

Keep in mind, he said this knowing that *I* am a mental health counselor. To make it more confusing as I reflect back on this comment, I distinctly remember a previous conversation in which he told me he used to see a therapist for anxiety and that it really helped him. Either way, his statement basically told me he thought my entire career was pointless.

THE FIRST DATE DRESS

I didn't respond at first, because I didn't want to get defensive and start an argument, but he must have picked up on my deliberate silence because he quickly asked if he offended me. I thought for a moment and eventually said, "No, that was just spoken like someone who has never experienced trauma." He seemed kind of taken aback and declared that he *had* indeed been through trauma. Then he asked if I wanted to hear about it, which of course I did.

In short, when he was a senior in high school, someone drugged him at a party, and he thought he was going crazy the next day at school***. He told me that he was eventually hospitalized, insisting he was in the hospital for a year, but that seemed odd to me, and even doctor friends of mine have confirmed that was highly unlikely given the situation.

*** I really wanted to ask how his parents didn't notice he was on a hallucinogen on a school morning, but I didn't think it would have been helpful.

Then, he told me the thing that—at least to me—made him sound a little like an uneducated conspiracy theorist. He said that the doctors kept giving him medication, but he had to tell them to stop because he knew they were actually making him worse. According to him "you just can't trust medical professionals." Cue shattering of any hope for a future together.

Now, I know that doctors are not infallible, but this blanket statement just made me cringe. I am genuinely glad that his experience with being drugged at a party is the worst thing he has ever gone through in his life, and I honestly hope that remains to be the case for him because he is a decent human being.

Later that evening, after we finished the last available episode of the *Game of Thrones* series, we had sex as per usual. However, this time, it was terrible. That was usually one of the better parts of our time together, and I just wasn't able to get into it. I am very confident that it was proof that I just can't be sexually attracted to someone who I don't think of as particularly bright.

After that night, I decided that I would end things the next time I saw him because even though he had never done anything wrong per se, things clearly weren't working out *and* now the sex was bad. I was acutely aware of the fact that this revelation coincidentally came after we had just finished watching *Game of Thrones*, and I hope he didn't think I was just using him for his HBO.

The next week, I invited GOTG over, and he clearly had no idea that I was going to end things. I told him that it didn't seem like anything was going to progress with us and that if I didn't see a future relationship with him then, I probably never would. He countered with the argument that I would feel differently if he had been *trying* to make me his girlfriend, because, you know, he would have taken me to nice dinners and stuff.

After a few more minutes of awkward discussion around the subject, he got up to leave, clearly disappointed. But before he walked out, he did present the offer that if I ever wanted a booty call, I could let him know. What an honor.

THE FIRST DATE DRESS

CHAPTER FIVE

New Year's Eve Guy

SHORTLY AFTER breaking things off with GoTG, I briefly stumbled back into my serial dating pattern, and I donned my olive-green dress for a few more insignificant first dates. Then, I simply gave up. I was so frustrated by the abundant lack of potential in a seemingly infinite pool of men to swipe through, and I was exhausted by my pursuit. I began to think that maybe my means of finding a partner was the real problem, so I deleted all of the dating apps from my phone, and I resolved to meet my person the old-fashioned way—IRL.

As evidenced by the story I'm about to tell, the apps were not solely responsible for my dating misadventures, but there are certainly aspects of online dating that are largely unappealing. In a lot of ways, dating apps are numbers games. You have to swipe right on more people than you actually want to talk to because only a portion of those people will match with you; you have to message more people than you want to meet up with because only a small percentage of those conversations will result in actual dates, and you have to meet up with more people than you would want to continue dating because an even smaller amount of those first dates will be a good fit romantically.

That means we have a lot of options but very few viable ones. The sheer idea of possibilities, however, can mean that people toss others aside much more quickly than they would if they had to go out into the world to secure their next date instead of haphazardly finding someone when they get bored and switch from Instagram to Bumble. With hundreds of people to swipe through, it can be extremely tempting to continue swiping and swiping, maybe even after you've met someone who you genuinely like, because there is always the promise that there could be something better out there if you only exercise your thumb a little longer.

I know I've fallen into a similar thought trap before, and there were certainly a few guys who didn't get a fair chance with me because I already had five other dates lined up that week, and maybe the guy I was going to meet on Friday would be better than the one sitting in front of me on Tuesday. Just the idea of another person who could potentially be a better fit meant that I was unable to invest in the present date.

Looking back, I think that was also a hearty dose of insecurity bursting forth. Part of the reason I was seeing so many people at the same time—other than the numbers game excuse—was imposter syndrome at its finest. At some point, these guys would surely realize they could find someone better, and if I was going on dates with multiple people, at least it wouldn't hurt as badly when one of them inevitably stopped dating me because he found a prettier, funnier, more interesting woman. If I had plenty of options, I wouldn't be alone. Well, I was indeed rarely alone, but I was often very lonely.

So, I renounced the online dating scene, and I paused my search for a partner. I needed a break because, quite frankly, I was exhausted. To my surprise, my much-needed hiatus was brief, cut short by meeting New Year's Eve Guy only four days after vowing to disembark the dating app train. Meaning that once again, I dismissed taking time to heal from my past relationship trauma, and I plunged right back into the possibility of someone who wanted me.

I was at my friend's 30th birthday party when I met New Year's Eve Guy (not on New Year's Eve). My friends and I were sitting around a firepit talking, and I noticed an attractive guy who had just arrived. I asked my friend if the guy in the plaid shirt was single, and when she confirmed that he was unattached, I requested an introduction. There was an immediate connection, and I knew he was someone I wanted to pursue.

Later in the evening, my friends decided to go for a swim in the freezing cold pool, but I chose to stay put for the warm fire and the cute guy. I moved to sit next to New Year's Eve Guy, and I noticed he was shivering, so I offered to share my blanket with him. He eagerly accepted, and we held hands in secret underneath a striped fleece. He stayed at the party significantly longer than he intended, and he didn't make a move to leave until I announced I was going home around midnight. He walked me to my car and asked for my number.

On my drive home, the painfully naïve voice in the back of my head started shouting, 'What a great story this would be! I finally abandoned my dating app ways, and four days later I met someone!' My sad belief in fate apparently translated into the delusion that I was living in a romantic comedy, and I was finally at the climax of the movie where things fall into place and I meet the right guy now that I have finally abandoned my hunt for true love.

Oh, Laura. When will you learn?

◆ ◆ ◆

A week later, New Year's Eve Guy and I went on our first date, and that was by far the best first date I had experienced since I started my dating tour. It was easy and comfortable, while still containing flashes of excitement as he reached for my hand. New Year's Eve Guy was the most seemingly well-adjusted person I had dated so far, and he checked almost every box on my excessive checklist.

After that night, New Year's Eve Guy and I started spending a lot of time together hanging out. And that is exactly what he called it, "hanging out." I should have known what that meant, especially given my experience with GoTG, but I still reserved hope, thinking it could one day evolve into a relationship. After all, he was "open" to whatever happened.

I did learn some positive things during my time with New Year's Eve Guy, and he particularly solidified how important it is to me to be with someone who is as physically active as I am. That was always something on my list—though it was towards the bottom—but I didn't realize how much I was craving that missing piece until New Year's Eve Guy planned a day for us to go cycling together. It was so simple. We rode our bikes around the city and ended up at the waterfront, taking a break to lie by the river and talk about life— our hands intertwined in the grass—before riding back to my place. That active date (no, I'm sorry, "hanging out" session) made my heart leap.

Despite the red flag vocabulary of "hanging out" and being "open," things actually seemed to be progressing with New Year's Eve Guy. We were texting every day and seeing each other a decent amount, our time often filled with thoughtful conversation. He even treated me to a nice dinner on my birthday. Later that month, he asked if I wanted to spend Christmas day together. Not exactly a casual holiday, right? It's not difficult to see why I believed he might actually want to date me in a significant way.

I was wrong.

The first big clue hinting towards his desire to remain casual came on a night that I was planning on going to a big caroling event in the city with a friend. I invited New Year's Eve

Guy to join us, and he told me he was already attending with his roommate but that we could meet up there. I was excited for us to meet each other's friends since we had been "hanging out" a little over a month at that point.

He was running late and kept texting me updates on his arrival time. When he let me know he was there, I sent him a picture of where I was standing so that he could find me in the crowd, and he responded by saying that he was in a different spot. When I asked if I should move to where he had settled, he didn't respond.

Much later in the evening, long after I returned home, he sent me a text asking if I had fun caroling. We were in the same place and could have easily seen each other, even for a few minutes, and he made no effort to walk a few feet to say hello. Then, he decided to completely skirt a potentially uncomfortable conversation by simply asking if I enjoyed the event. Much to his displeasure, I'm sure, I asked about what happened and expressed my disappointment.

As simple as that sounds, it was a huge moment of growth for me. I didn't get overly emotional about it, even though the situation was kind of shitty, *and* I vocalized my concern in a rational, mature way. In the past, I would not have even voiced that I was bothered, and I would have let it slowly churn in my system until I eventually erupted, vomiting feelings all over the place.

I had learned in past relationships to keep my mouth shut because if I did express unhappiness with something the other person did, somehow it would be turned around on me. He couldn't possibly have any flaws, so the situation had to be my fault, and my resulting feelings were simply wrong. In fact, I found *myself* apologizing in instances where I should have been receiving an apology, because it was easier to take the blame and avoid the other person yelling at me, or worse, totally ignoring me. When you're trained to hate pieces of yourself, it's easy to lose the ability to stand up for what you deserve.

But at this time, I responded appropriately, finally not letting my past experiences totally shape my emotional reactions. In turn, New Year's Eve Guy explained that he felt weird about introducing girls he's "hanging out" with to his friends too soon. I accepted this explanation without debate, although a part of me still couldn't comprehend why he had suggested meeting up in the first place and why he continued to update me on his arrival if he didn't have any intentions to actually see me. I still didn't catch on that he did not foresee anything serious emerging between us.

Even with a few questions lingering in the air, I let it go, and we decided to see each other when he got back in town after visiting his family in another state. Sadly, he had to extend his trip after his father was hospitalized. We ended up not being able to spend Christmas together because he was still away, so instead, we made plans to see each other on New Year's Eve.

When he was back in town, New Year's Eve Guy immediately had to work night shifts, so we waited until December 31st to see each other. A few days before New Year's Eve, he told me he was sick and asked if I wouldn't mind watching the ball drop on tv at his apartment if he wasn't feeling better. I let him know that I was more than happy to do that. Now, in hindsight, I'm pretty sure he fabricated his illness in the hopes that I would say no to staying in on New Year's Eve. That way, he could go out with his friends and not have to bring me along.

The night of New Year's Eve, he texted me and told me he was feeling better. His friend who lived in his building invited him over, and he invited me to join. I, of course, said yes. Then, at about 8:45pm, I received a message from him informing me that his friend had tickets to a party downtown, but he didn't have one for me to tag along.

I was livid.

Thankfully, I reigned in my anger enough to respond rationally, but I still thought it was pretty awful of him to cancel plans with me at the last minute on New Year's Eve. I could have made plans with friends, but instead, I was going to start 2019 on my couch watching Netflix alone.

He apologized, and I accepted the apology.

A few hours later, I changed my mind about staying in, and I decided that I still wanted to have a midnight kiss as planned. After all, New Year's Eve Guy and I were clearly not in an exclusive relationship. So, I went on a dating app and sent a message to someone who I had been chatting with prior to deleting the app to see if he was available. He was downtown with his friends, but he said that he would be happy for me to come join him.

Clearly, the hot-mess version of me was in full swing as I got dressed, summoned a Lyft, and headed downtown to kiss a stranger at midnight on New Year's Eve. Making that deadline, however, seemed unlikely when my ride was reassigned four times. After sitting in an astronomical amount of traffic, I arrived downtown with barely any time to spare. My kiss was waiting just on the other side of the busiest part of downtown, where our version of the ball drops at midnight, meaning I had to shove my way through a wall of humans. As I squeezed through the massive crowd, I reached a very small break in people, so I broke into a run since it was already 11:56pm.

I dashed forward and collided hard with another person. As I looked up to apologize, I realized that it was New Year's Eve Guy who I just forcibly ran into with my shoulder. Really? Really? In a crowd of *thousands* of people, I

PHYSICALLY RAN INTO THE ONE GUY WHO BLEW ME OFF. I can't make this shit up.

We looked at each other incredulously for what seemed like 10 minutes—but was realistically only 30 seconds—before he asked what I was doing downtown. I matter of factly informed him that I was meeting a guy from Hinge since he blew me off. He looked a little hurt and asked if I was still going to meet my Hinge date. I answered his question with another question, asking if he wanted me to go or stay. He answered with an ambivalent shrug and simply said that we were standing in a perfect place to watch the midnight festivities. It was 11:59pm. I stayed and kissed him at midnight.

After the initial "Happy New Year"

exclamations dissolved, we turned to each other in a standstill, neither of us sure how to proceed. He broke the silence by saying, "Hey, at least you didn't catch me with another girl?" How nice of him to offer me that comfort.

He again asked if I was going to meet up with the dating app guy and refused to give a straight answer about his feelings when I once more tossed the question back to him. Eventually, it was decided that I would go meet up with Hinge Guy, New Year's Eve Guy would go to his party, and if I felt unsafe, I would text him, and we could meet up again. He even made a big show of taking his phone off of silent so that he wouldn't miss a text from me and offered for me to stay at his place later, which was within walking distance. We exchanged awkward goodbyes and walked away.

What I craved most in that instant was to hear him say that he didn't want me to be with anyone else. I wanted that movie moment in which he realizes that he might be losing an amazing girl and fights to keep her. I wanted him to suddenly care.

The hard truth is that there is nothing I could have done or said to make him unexpectedly become more invested. And, the fact that he wasn't pursuing more does not actually determine anything about my worth as a person. At the time, of course, I thought it had everything to do with my lack of desirability.

When I met up with the guy from Hinge, I was immediately overwhelmed by creepy vibes. There wasn't anything in particular he did that would warrant me feeling so uncomfortable,

THE FIRST DATE DRESS

but I know most women can relate to that strong intuition saying that something isn't quite right.

I only spent about ten minutes with Hinge Guy before making up an excuse to leave. Shortly after, I realized that he was following me. I texted New Year's Eve Guy saying that the guy I met up with was a creep, that he was following me through the streets, and that I didn't feel safe. I asked if we could meet up since he had offered that as an option.

While I waited for New Year's Eve Guy to respond, I spotted an elderly couple standing outside of a restaurant and asked if I could talk to them for a few minutes because I was being followed. They warmly agreed to pretend to know me, and I am still so appreciative of their kindness. Once it seemed like Hinge Guy was gone, I continued my journey, heading toward a busy street corner that felt safer to await New Year's Eve Guy's response.

I waited an hour and a half on that corner before I realized that he was not going to text me back. At almost 2am, I paid $70 for an Uber home, sitting with the question of whether or not I will ever be enough for someone. That's how I started the new year.

The next afternoon, I still had not heard from New Year's Eve Guy, and I finally resigned all hope for our romance. Regardless of whether or not we were going to continue seeing each other, he should have responded at some point to make sure I was safe, and his lack of basic decency was the last straw for me. I mean, if the last message I received from literally anybody I know was that they were alone downtown being following by a sketchy person, I could not fathom not checking in to see if they made it home.

My mind swirled with thoughts that I would be alone forever*. I was further convinced that no one would ever want me, and I took a significant step back in the small progress I had made toward recognizing my worth. I am embarrassed by the amount of time I spent allowing the actions of a man to dictate how I felt about myself. Continuing in my unhealthy cycle, I once again wanted a man to want me even if I no longer wanted him.

It felt like the world was ending, but it actually had nothing to do with him. It wasn't because I had strong feelings for him or liked him any more than I had liked any of the other

---

* Yes, hella dramatic, but it was how it felt at the time.

guys I had dated. It was because, to me, the failure of yet another dating scenario was clearly a reflection of my inability to attract a partner who would want me exactly as I was.

Later that day, I texted New Year's Eve Guy. I told him that I really enjoyed our time together but that it didn't feel as if things were going anywhere. His response actually seemed extremely genuine when he told me that he wasn't ready for a relationship with anyone and that while he had tried to open up to me, he wasn't in a place where he could. At the time, I couldn't believe that was true, but now I can see that it was probably the honest answer. He had talked a decent amount about an ex that I don't think he ever healed from, and as I reflect on my time with him, I think that he was trying to allow himself to be vulnerable with me but simply couldn't.

New Year's Eve Guy's only crime was not being ready for commitment, which unfortunately manifested itself in the form of him blowing me off on a major holiday instead of just communicating with me about it like an adult. Still, he was a huge improvement from the other guys I had been seeing.

If I had chosen to see it that way instead of allowing the letdown to define me, I think the next chapter in my dating journey (which also happens to be the next chapter in this book) wouldn't have been quite so disastrous. Because, now at this point, my self-worth is at an all-time low. Through the floor. Subterranean.

CHAPTER SIX

Narcissistic Guy

IN MANY WAYS, this chapter is a turning point in my story. This is where I hit rock bottom with such a spectacular crash that the only direction in which I can possibly travel is up. If you have ever dated someone with traits often associated with Narcissistic Personality Disorder, you may identify with my gradual, unknowing descent into the abyss.

For those of you who haven't had such a magical experience, I'll give a brief rundown of narcissists: Initially, they are exceptionally charming. The beginning stages of dating a narcissist are delightful, because people with narcissistic characteristics are good at being attentive and charismatic, and they certainly know what to say and do to make you swoon.

Then, things start to change—subtly at first—so you barely notice. They begin to test boundaries to see what you are willing to endure and just how far they can push before manipulating you with words and actions to guarantee you stick around longer. Each time they succeed, they raise the stakes. Narcissists aren't big on empathy, which is exemplified by their concentrated focus on their own needs and wants. Everything absolutely has to be on the narcissist's terms, including when you see each other and in what capacity, because narcissists get off on being in control. They are not as important as they believe themselves to be.

The narcissist's dream partner is someone with tremendously low self-worth because people lacking self-esteem are more willing to stick around when they aren't being treated well *and* they are more easily manipulated by gestures that are designed to show that the other person finds them worthy (because they don't see that worth in themselves).

It's no surprise then that I was the ideal candidate for Narcissistic Guy. I'm not diagnosing him with Narcissistic Personality Disorder because I'm not his therapist, but I will say that he meets enough criteria according to the DSM-V. Regardless of what label suits him best, my feelings were manipulated and tossed around like a child's plaything for about a month and a half until I reached a point where I finally rebounded off of the bottommost place I could land and started to ascend back up, eventually reclaiming my identity.

The scary thing is that many narcissists aren't even aware that their grandiose views of themselves do not align with how others see them, and those who do possess some supply of awareness simply don't care. I'm sure that the guy I'm about to tell you about would be shocked, appalled, and offended to know I even equated him with a narcissist.

Narcissistic Guy and I matched on Bumble about a month after I called it quits with New Year's Eve Guy*. In the interim, I went on a few dates with other guys, and there was one person

---

* My break from the app scene was clearly short-lived.

who I liked and could see myself dating (primarily because he fit every ounce of my checklist). That guy didn't feel a spark, and we never made it to a third date. With the disappointment of rejection dangling over my head, my belief that no one would ever want me escalated, leaving me in the prime position to be manipulated with meaningless affirmations and false promises.

The first two weeks with Narcissistic Guy were honestly pretty great, which I guess is why I didn't foresee what was coming later. Our first date lasted six and a half hours, and we spent that entire time talking about our lives and getting to know each other on what seemed to be a real, deep level.

Because the universe likes to sprinkle humor into my life, Neck Guy happened to be eating dinner at the restaurant where Narcissistic Guy and I were drinking margaritas, so I shared the hickey story with my date, and I semi-joked that I was pondering writing a book recounting my dating stories. Little did he know that I would one day write that book and that he would have such a significant chapter in it.

There were certainly some "too much too soon" tendencies from both of us, and we went on four dates in the first week of seeing each other. One of my friends attempted to point out that this was something I had previously identified as a red flag, but I was convinced that the situation with Narcissistic Guy was different. I rationalized the volume of dates in such a short time by thinking of it as consolidating two weeks' worth of dates into one because I was going to be out of town the following week. That makes it okay, right?

Wrong.

Following our first date, Narcissistic Guy consistently texted me every day, sending different variations of, "Have a great day pretty lady!" My friend joked that he always referred to me as "pretty lady" because he didn't want to get his women confused. Looking back, I'm not convinced she was entirely wrong.

Even amidst the abundance of attentiveness, there were a few times in that first week that he didn't follow through on plans, citing a misunderstanding as the reasoning. I was so set on things working out that I convinced myself that he was right about what had happened. You'll see later on that these "misunderstandings" became more frequent and the excuses became less believable.

The last night I was in town before leaving on my trip happened to be Valentine's Day, and I remember thinking it was sweet that we had a date planned that evening, despite the fact that we hadn't even known each other for a full week. He brought a single red rose and a chocolate bar when he picked me up from my house before taking me to dinner. *Swoon.* We had a great night, and on my flight the next morning, I once again fell into daydreams about what this could become.

While I was away, Narcissistic Guy texted me regularly to tell me he missed me, continuing to refer to me as "pretty lady," and we talked on the phone for a few hours most nights. I was floating in a pool of affection and attention. That pool, however, would slowly transform into one in which I almost drowned as it filled with manipulation and avoidance.

Narcissistic Guy offered to pick me up from the airport when I returned from my trip. *Swoon, swoon, swoon.* This was without a doubt too soon for such a gesture—but I embraced it all the same because it showed that he wanted to be with me. After he picked me up, he stayed over at my place, but we didn't have sex because he "didn't want to rush things." *Swoon.*

The first turn of events happened that weekend when we foolishly decided to spend approximately 36 hours together. Yes, we knew each other for two weeks and we spent *36 continuous hours* in each other's company. On the second night of our never-ending date, Narcissistic Guy started pushing for us to go out for a drink because he needed to tell me something, and alcohol was his necessary assistant. After he was intoxicated enough to share his secret, he dropped a bit of a bomb on me.

Apparently, Narcissistic Guy had a kid. He hadn't had any contact with his child in years, but he wanted to eventually fight for partial custody. There was no part of me at the time that was yearning to be a mom-figure, so my already irrational thoughts about our future shattered ever so slightly. He went on to tell me how badly he was treated by the mother of his child and her parents, and he was the ultimate victim in his tale. There are parts of the story that seemed exaggerated to me, and now I wonder how much of it was true and how much of it was filtered through the lens of a narcissist.

Even after receiving that news, I was ready to make things work. I was determined to have a successful relationship with someone who wanted me, even if he didn't quite fit what I thought I wanted. Maybe I didn't know what I wanted after all? I had only known this guy for two weeks, and I already was willing to readjust my mindset to fit in with what *he* wanted. I guess that's what happens when you don't see anything inherently good about yourself.

I drank way more gin and tonics than I should have that night, and when we arrived back at my place, I completely threw myself at him in the most embarrassing fashion. He turned me down, saying he didn't want to take advantage of me, although I think his rejection was partially because he wanted sex to be his decision, not mine. I went to sleep a little hurt but also happy that he was being such a gentleman.

In the middle of the night, he cuddled up next to me and put his leg on top of me. It was heavy, so I gently pushed away his leg, and I fell back asleep. When I woke up about an hour later, he was gone. I was completely puzzled, and that confusion didn't dissipate when I found him asleep on my couch, his feet dangling over the edge as it was way too small for his body. When he woke up later, he told me he moved to the sofa because I had "pushed him away."

Instead of recognizing the level of drama in that response, I apologized, terrified that he would change his mind about me if I didn't act perfectly. Still caught up in the fear of being alone, I did not refuse his advances to fuck me that morning, even though my feelings were still tangled in a ball after the previous night's happenings.

If I'm being honest, the sex wasn't very good, and I'm not saying that just because I don't currently like or respect this person. In addition to it not being very enjoyable for me, it also ended pretty abruptly, once again leaving me confused. Later, I pieced together what probably had happened.

When we tried to switch positions, it wasn't a smooth transition (as it rarely is), so I playfully laughed at our inability to successfully turn over. He pulled away immediately after that. While I don't think there is any research to back this up, I'm fairly confident that the quickest way to get a narcissist to stop having sex with you is to laugh during sex. He probably thought I was laughing *at him*; therefore, he had to punish me by withdrawing.

I sat in a puddle of perplexity as we cuddled for a few minutes before he announced that he had to leave. I felt as if I had been riding an emotional roller coaster, and I was being suddenly thrown out at the top of it. Because of that, I unquestionably started acting weird and distant, but when he asked me what was wrong, I lied and said that everything was okay.

Shortly after leaving, Narcissistic Guy texted me to see what was going on, and I ended up telling him that I slept with him before I was really ready for it. Then, I confided in him that sometimes I subconsciously use my sexuality as a way to ensure someone will continue to like me, which was a realization I had only just made for myself. Ten hours later, he still hadn't responded.

By the time I realized he never acknowledged my message, I was out drinking with one of my friends, and I guess a secondary lesson I learned from this chapter is that I should not drink heavily when I'm upset. I spiraled speedily downward, and I sent incredulous text messages calling him out on not responding to what I thought was such significant content. When I wasn't satisfied with the half-hearted answer I received from him 30 minutes later, I told him I was done. Obviously, this was not my finest moment.

Despite the levels of drunk, crazy person pouring out of my messages, he said he didn't want things to be over, and we decided to meet up the following night to talk about it. When we saw each other, he seemed pretty understanding of what I was feeling when I sent those texts, especially given that I slept with him before I was emotionally ready to do so, which was compounded by the fact that he left immediately after. Since he was being kind, I decided to share some deeper emotions, and I told him about the insecurities I had been feeling about myself. I told him that I didn't feel particularly beautiful or special, and he didn't really give much of a response. I didn't realize at the time that I was giving him ammunition.

The rest of that night went well, and once again, I ignored potential problems because I wanted a person to love me. We made plans to see each other a few days later and pretended as if the last few days never happened.

In the following days, Narcissistic Guy sent me multiple texts saying that he missed me and that he was sad that we hadn't seen each other in a few days. We once again solidified our plans for the next day.

When that day arrived, however, I asked him about our plans, and he told me he was going to be with a friend for a little while. I inquired about when he would be free, and three hours later, he still hadn't responded. I messaged him again, trying absurdly hard to not be bothersome, and I asked if he could let me know what time we were getting together so I could figure out my schedule. Immediately after my second text, he let me know that he wouldn't be able to see me after all.

I tried to calmly express that my feelings were hurt. Fully knowing that one of my biggest pet peeves is people cancelling plans at the last minute, he did it anyway and left me hanging for hours while I waited for him to reply. I sent that message at 7:23pm. He responded 15 hours later at 10:16am.

That text the next morning was, of course, very apologetic. He explained that his phone died and that he was sorry I "got neglected." Even though I was upset, I accepted the apology and once again tried to be super cool about the whole thing. After that, he continued to send me messages saying how much he missed me, but it proved difficult to set any actual plans. Almost a week passed since the night he blew me off, and I was having trouble understanding why he wasn't trying to see me when he was so intently and consistently telling me how much he couldn't wait to be with me again.

Eventually, I asked if we could meet up because I was starting to feel as if he wasn't into me anymore. He told me that he had missed a big deadline and was scrambling to fix things but that he would see me later that night despite his elevated stress levels because he wanted to work things out. In true narcissistic fashion, he could see me ever so slightly slipping away, and he said the one thing that without a doubt would manipulate me into sticking around longer. He said, "I care about you. You're a priority, and I'll start showing you that."

Narcissistic Guy knew that I had never felt as if I were a priority in any of my previous relationships, and that line was like a golden ticket back into my heart. I immediately forgot all of the doubts that had been brewing, and we made plans to see each other that night.

An hour before we were going to meet up, he told me he couldn't make it.

Clearly, I wasn't happy. I gave a feeble ultimatum by expressing that if he didn't talk to me about what was going on, even if it was just a phone conversation, I would start to seriously question things. He asked me to call him the next morning, and he profusely apologized. Narcissistic Guy was apparently still dealing with the deadline he had missed, and he talked about his own struggles so much that by the time we hung up, I had apologized for adding to his stress. After a few more days of "hey pretty lady" texts, we made another attempt to develop plans.

At the time this was happening, I had started reading Sue Johnson's book *Hold Me Tight*, to which I can attribute a significant portion of my growth as a person. The book is based on Emotionally Focused Therapy, which has roots in attachment theory, and Johnson writes about the unhealthy patterns romantic partners fall into as well as how to step out of them. As I read her book, I realized that I 1000% needed to work on how I approached relationships when I felt as if a secure bond was being broken so that I could be healthier for my partner and myself.

I started incorporating some of the concepts in *Hold me Tight* when I was interacting with Narcissistic Guy after we spoke on the phone that morning. I began to identify and communicate underlying emotions in a calm and rational way. I was understanding and kind when he cited stress as the reason we weren't seeing each other. I was being a better version of myself. I had learned essential skills, but I was practicing them on the wrong person.

When we did finally see each other in person, Narcissistic Guy was once again apologetic and swore he would make things up to me. He had to briefly travel out of town, and he asked if he could take me to dinner the night he returned from his trip.

Of course, I would have wholeheartedly agreed to that plan regardless of any other factors, but the idea of a relaxing night with him sounded even better because I knew I was going to be dealing with an exceptionally anxiety-producing situation the day before.

My dad was diagnosed with cancer a few months earlier, and he was scheduled to have his bladder removed while Narcissistic Guy was away. Theoretically, the proposed dinner would have been celebratory, because if the surgery was successful, that meant my dad would be cancer-free.

However, his surgery never happened. The cancer had permeated my dad's bladder and spread too far for it to ever be surgical. The only moment that has rivaled the pain I felt when I heard that news was when I received the call that my dad passed away seven months later.

Because that day was so challenging, I didn't reach out to anyone, although my amazing friends continuously messaged and called me to check in. I didn't hear from Narcissistic Guy at all that day, even though he knew my dad was supposed to be undergoing major surgery. When I did hear from him the following morning, I told him what had happened, and his messages to me were very kind and supportive. I told him I was happy he was coming home that day, and he said he was too.

As dinnertime approached, I had a feeling gnawing at my gut saying that he was going to once again cancel our plans, but my brain countered, thinking he wouldn't possibly do that on a day that I was struggling so much. I learned to always listen to my gut.

I asked Narcissistic Guy if we were still having

dinner together, and this was our conversation:

Me: Still on for dinner?

Narcissistic Guy: I'm not getting in til laaaate :-(

Me: Oh, I thought we had made plans. I guess I misunderstood.

Narcissistic Guy: Yeah. It's my fault. I wasn't planning on getting back so late :(

Me: I really needed you tonight. How late are you getting in?

Me (two hours later): Do you have time to call me before your flight? It's been a rough day, and it would be nice to hear your voice.

13 hours later

114

Narcissistic Guy: I'm so sorry lady! Phone died in the airport and I got in late! I hope you're doing ok. I'd like to see you tonight.

Okay, let's break this down a little. First of all, he wouldn't have been at the airport at 5pm if his flight wasn't until 9pm. Second, if he was at the airport absurdly early, *and* his phone was about to die, *and* he didn't pack a charger, he could have given me a heads up that his phone was at 1%, especially given the nature of our conversation. Finally, if upon his arrival home he magically summoned his ride without a functional phone, he could have texted when he plugged his phone in at home instead of waiting until the following morning. And we can't forget that this was the second time he used the excuse of his phone dying in order to avoid an uncomfortable conversation.

I still agreed to see him that night.

As usual, he was kind and apologetic when we met up, and, as usual, everything was on his terms. He switched up our meeting time to one that wasn't convenient for me, he encouraged me to bail on plans with my friend, and he changed the place from the one I initially suggested. But still, I went, and I hoped that if I could continue working on myself, he would continue to want me. If I could just be better than I was, I would deserve to be treated better by him.

I persevered in my determination to make things work, and a few nights later, I offered to bring him soup because he wasn't feeling well. We had a nice, low-key evening together until his friend called asking if he could check on her child who was home alone and having an allergic reaction.

Narcissistic Guy asked if I could drive the two of us over to his friend's house, and shortly after we arrived, his friend showed up as well. Her daughter was fine, and I awkwardly stood there as they talked, feeling slightly invisible until she finally introduced herself. He initiated no introductions, which I found to be strange.

We went back to his place to watch a movie and fell asleep on the couch. The next morning, he asked about my plans for the day, and I told him that I had to teach an exercise class before going to my friend's St. Patrick's Day parade party. He seemed offended when he asked why he wasn't invited to the party. I explained that he was welcome to join me and that I hadn't invited him because he was sick, so I assumed he wouldn't want to come. He assured me he did.

As I was on my way to the party, I texted him to give the address, and he informed me that he went to meet up with some of his friends instead. I shared my location with him so that he could say hello if he happened to be in the same area, but he didn't respond.

He was, however, in the same area, because after the parade ended, I saw him walking down the street with a group of people. I called out his name—excited to see him—and he looked slightly bewildered when he noticed me, as if he had been caught doing something he wasn't supposed to do. He didn't introduce me to any of the people with him, and he was speaking to me as if he barely knew me.

I asked if he would be able to hang out later, and he said that he would text me that night. Then, he walked away from me, leaving me slightly intoxicated and alone in the middle of the bustling street, donning an emerald green boa and a bruised ego. Of course, I never heard from him that night.

I was getting closer and closer to ending things, but there was a small part of me that was still hoping he would turn things around and fight for me. I was so desperate for someone—for anyone—to care for me that I simply couldn't help myself.

The next day, Narcissistic Guy sent me a "hey pretty lady" message, and since I was with a friend, I didn't respond for a few hours. He then proceeded to express he was worried about my well-being and texted again to make sure I was okay because he cared so much about me. When I told my friend what happened, she immediately advised me to end things. I am

THE FIRST DATE DRESS

embarrassed to say that in response I showed her his text, and I naïvely said, "But look at this! He does care!"

Oh, Laura. Oh, sweet girl. Please get your head out of your ass.

I almost heeded my friend's advice, but instead of fully committing to a healthy decision of splitting from Narcissistic Guy, I resolved to offer him one final chance.

Narcissistic Guy asked if he could see me the following night, and I told him that I would see him, but only if he came over to my place early in the evening. He quickly agreed, again acting appropriately the instant he felt me pulling back from him.

As evening approached, I suggested 7pm as a meeting time, and he informed me that he had to help his friend move some "stuff" and that he would understand if I would rather reschedule for the following evening. When I said I wouldn't be free again until the weekend, he replied, "Nooo. I wanna seee yooou."

THEN, FUCKING SEE ME. IF YOU MISS ME AND CARE ABOUT ME AND WANT TO SPEND TIME WITH ME, THEN SEE ME, STICK TO PLANS YOU MAKE WITH ME, AND STOP TREATING ME LIKE GARBAGE, YOU NARCISSISTIC ASSHOLE.

I unexpectedly felt something shift inside of me. A new view of the situation began to settle down and make itself comfortable in my mind. In that moment, instead of feeling as if I would never be loved, instead of feeling a desire to beg someone to stay, instead of feeling like I was deficient in some significant way, I thought, 'Well, I know I deserve better than this crap.'

Despite that thought's simplicity, it was the impetus for my deliberate rise back out of the ravine of insecurity which almost stole me away from myself.

Not surprisingly, I decided to end things with Narcissistic Guy. I asked if he could stop by my house after he was done helping his friend because I wanted to talk to him about something. He "couldn't handle" that because apparently, I had "said enough." Sensing the looming manipulation, I asked what he was referencing, seeing as I only asked if we could talk. He then insisted that he "didn't need a goodbye conversation" because he "didn't need to feel any worse" than he already did.

At this point, I was so done, but I wanted closure. I have a tendency to prefer wrapping my endings in nice little bows before sending them into the world, but, true to someone with narcissistic tendencies, he wouldn't give me that satisfaction. So, of course, he ignored my next text message.

In my insane need to have a definitive conclusion to our tumultuous time together, I called him three times, not caring if he thought I was crazy, because there was not an ounce of me that still desired him.

When Narcissistic Guy didn't answer, I sent one more text message, distributing a few placating, trite sentiments in a final attempt to get him to talk to me. I said that he was a "great guy" and that I was sorry that I "wasn't enough" for him, not meaning either statement. I am fully aware that this was ridiculous, but at the time I was convinced that I needed to have a conversation with him in order to feel better about the situation. When I didn't hear back, I resigned myself to the idea that I would not get closure. Instead, I would start to take tentative steps into my new-found sense of self.

Two days later, Narcissistic Guy's name flashed across my phone, accompanied by the following missive:

I'm sorry it took a few days to process. I have a lot on my plate including surgery tomorrow**. I

** He was having a small growth removed.

just can't handle drama. Sitting down to have serious discussions, blowing up my phone, saying you're not enough for me. I'd like to continue this. I would. I would need help with my current stresses, they are very temporary. I don't need more stress. If you think that's possible, I'd like to continue.

I still cannot believe he sent a paragraph insisting that he was stressed and needed help with that when a week earlier I learned that my dad was dying. Sorry, but having a growth removed from your back and missing a deadline for school do not compare in any way to the stress that accompanies the impending death of a parent. The lack of empathy was astounding.

But, of course, Narcissistic Guy said he couldn't handle drama. That's why he was ultimately dramatic in refusing to have an adult conversation. That's why he constantly rearranged and cancelled plans. That's why he avoided responding to important texts and fabricated stories about his phone dying. All drama must be reserved for him and him alone.

I wanted so badly to respond to his message. I wanted to call him out for the discrepancies between his words and his actions. I wanted to tell him I had no interest in ever seeing or talking to him again. But, what would have been the point? I was already moving forward—despite the way I was treated—and I did not need to waste any more of my time communicating with him.

I simply didn't answer.

My response instead was to make an agreement with myself that I would never again put myself in that position. I swore that I would not allow another man to make me feel unworthy, and, more importantly, I promised that I would find a way to make sure *I* didn't make myself feel unworthy either.

THE FIRST DATE DRESS

CHAPTER SEVEN

St. Patty's Day Guy

After Narcissistic Guy left me alone in the middle of the street on St. Patrick's Day, I continued on with my friends and declared a new mission for the night: I would find a hot guy, make out with him, and never see him again*. Of course, because I'm me, I set my goal and then dated the aforementioned "hot guy"

---

* Narcissistic Guy had previously made it clear we weren't exclusively dating.

129

for the next three months**.

We ended up at a St. Patrick's Day parade afterparty, and I spotted St. Patty's Day Guy immediately. My friends and I nodded in agreement with the silent understanding that he would be the perfect guy to meet the task at hand. I found myself naturally engaged in conversation with him, initially talking about health and nutrition—a mutual passion of ours. He told me that he used to be a bodybuilder, and I didn't need to question it given that his biceps were as big as my head. At some point, we realized that we were standing alone in a courtyard, and we had no idea when the others left because we had been so entranced by our conversation and apparent chemistry.

St. Patty's Day Guy and I found our friends inside, and they declared we were going out to a neighborhood bar. I had stopped drinking a few

---

** Ironically never reaching exclusivity with him either

hours earlier so that I could drive home, but my friend encouraged me to have another drink and stay over at her place across the street. I drank just enough that I would need to take her up on her offer; however, about an hour later, St. Patty's Day Guy pointed out that my friends had abandoned me.

Thankfully, St. Patty's Day Guy was a decent guy and didn't take advantage of the situation. He asked if we could stay and talk until I sobered up, so we continued our conversation for the next few hours at the bar before he took me to dinner[*].

I told him all about Narcissistic Guy, and even though he admitted to being biased by his attraction to me, he gave his honest opinion on the situation, which of course was that I should dump Narcissistic Guy immediately. He even

---

[*] Ironically at the same restaurant where I had my first date with Narcissistic Guy and spotted Neck Guy

pulled a phone charger out of his pocket and said, "Seriously, no one's phone dies in 2019."

After offering to pay for my quesadilla, St. Patty's Day Guy walked me to my car, asked for my number, and kissed me goodnight. There was electricity from the start. About 20 minutes later, he texted to make sure I made it home safely. There was also kindness from the start.

Two days later—and a few hours before I officially ended things with Narcissistic Guy— St. Patty's Day Guy called me to ask if he could take me to dinner. Like, actually called me on the phone. What?? Who still does that? I was already noticing such vast differences between him and Narcissistic Guy that I quickly agreed to his date proposal.

Our first date was lovely. He treated me to dinner at an adorable little French restaurant, and then we went to a local dive bar to play pool. Before we started the game, I was playfully trash talking because I used to play pool daily with my family, but I failed to remember that I was about 10 years old the last time I held a pool stick. Seeing my distress from realizing I was so bad at it, St. Patty's Day Guy threw the game just enough that I didn't feel terrible about my lousy pool-playing abilities, but not so much that I actually won.

St. Patty's Day Guy and I continued to go on dates[***], and we began to develop a solid friendship in addition to our strong physical chemistry. When I found myself needing a date to a work gala event, he offered to accompany me, even though he wouldn't know anybody, and we had just begun seeing each other.

The night of the event, St. Patty's Day Guy

[***] Including attending a paranormal circus, which may be the weirdest date I've ever been on

was over thirty minutes late picking me up, and I was annoyed because I had arranged a pre-gala gathering with my work friends that I would partially miss. He was apologetic, and we ended up having a good time, so I let it go. A few days later, my boss asked if my date to the gala bought a new suit for the event because she noticed that the threads on the back hadn't been cut. I'm still not sure if that was true, but I have a suspicion that St. Patty's Day Guy was late picking me up because he was buying a suit. If that was the case, it was quite possibly one of the sweetest things any guy had ever done for me.

It felt wonderful to be with someone who made an effort and who truly wanted to know me. More importantly, it felt amazing to not need those things in order to feel good about myself. I was continuously working on my self-esteem issues, and—even though I often sought reassurance from St. Patty's Day Guy—I slowly found enough worth in myself that I could be okay with or without him.

There's a decent chance that I might still be with St. Patty's Day Guy today if a few major events hadn't taken place, but obviously things didn't work out since there's another chapter after this one.

For a few months, I had been considering moving to another state, although I wasn't planning on leaving for another year. When I told St. Patty's Day Guy that I was likely going to move at some point, he told me that he wasn't tied to the city we were in either and that if things progressed with us, he wouldn't be opposed to living somewhere else.

Almost three months into dating St. Patty's Day Guy, I was offered an amazing work opportunity on the opposite side of the country, and even though the transition was significantly sooner than I anticipated, I was excited by the prospect. St. Patty's Day Guy was extremely supportive at first. He even started making comments like, "Who knows? Maybe I'll end up moving too." He seemed genuinely happy for me.

When I officially accepted the position, however, things started to change. A few days after I told him I was definitely moving, St. Patty's Day Guy and I had plans to spend an entire day together, and he supremely blew me off, which was extremely out of character for him. He said he wasn't in a good headspace but didn't offer any more substance to his excuse.

I—having recently resolved to not put up with any more bullshit from men—almost ended things then. However, I consulted a few friends, and they pointed out that I seemed to be vacillating between the two extremes of giving too many chances and not giving any. I had to remind myself that there is no perfect person, and one instance like that should not negate months of being treated well. Even though this wasn't a situation where things worked out, that was an important realization.

When we met up for coffee a few days later, things felt different. St. Patty's Day Guy was acting distant, and he was having a hard time articulating what was going on in his mind. He was usually a pretty decent communicator, but that characteristic wasn't shining through on that particular day.

I happened to be flying to Turkey later that week for a ten-day vacation, and we agreed to see each other when I was back in the country. With an awkward goodbye hug, we parted. On my trip, I reflected on the situation and decided it would be best for both of us to end things when I got back instead of dragging out another month and a half of potential weirdness before I moved away.

The day I flew back, St. Patty's Day Guy texted me to welcome me home. We exchanged messages for the next few days, but we made no moves to see each other, even though I was about to leave on another, much shorter, trip. Finally, he asked if we could meet up, but I already had plans. I refused to rearrange my time with my friends for a man as I was so accustomed to doing in the past.

Looking back, I realize I could have initiated a meetup instead of leaving that responsibility entirely in his hands, especially since I was considering ending things. I was so used to him taking the lead, and I held onto just enough insecurities that I feared he would think I was needy if I reached out first. This was the perfect example of how I reverted back to my old ways of caring what a guy thought of me even if I wasn't sure I still wanted to be with him. I would rather wait for him to ask to see me than dare have him think I was eager for his attention.

As women, societal expectations tell us to never come across as needy or desperate, and many of us hold back with men in order to come across as cool and laidback. Now, I know that the right person won't be turned off by me texting or calling first and certainly won't think less of me for expressing my thoughts and feelings without being prompted. Maybe if I came to that realization sooner, things with St. Patty's Day Guy would have ended differently.

When I told St. Patty's Day Guy that I would be busy on the day he asked to see me, I received the following response:

Oh, okay. Maybe it's best we just move on then.

After three months of going on dates, after sharing deep aspects of our personal lives, after investing an abundance of time and energy, he said we should move on in a succinct text message.

I responded by saying that I was starting to think the same thing but that I at least wanted to have an in-person conversation about it after all we had experienced together. In response, he essentially told me to have a nice life. I wished him the best, and I figured I would never hear from him again. It hurt, but it did not define me.

Of course, I heard from him a few hours later, apologizing for the way he handled things, and he asked to meet up that night. I couldn't see him that evening, so we left the conversation with question marks hanging in the air.

I decided that since I was moving in a month and a half, I would forget about St. Patty's Day Guy and find a casual dating partner, something easy and care-free before I began my new life.

I returned to the dating apps in search of such an arrangement, and I saw St. Patty's Day Guy on Tinder. We had both deleted our dating profiles, even though we were never officially in an exclusive relationship, but it didn't take either of us long to hop back onto the apps. I swiped right on him—mostly because I was curious to see if he would swipe right too—and we matched. He sent me a message on Tinder that said "Hi." I sent a laughing emoji. Then, we had no contact for another month.

I did find someone on Bumble to "hang out" with until my move, and you'll get to read about him in the following chapter. However, my story with St. Patty's Day Guy isn't quite over.

About a month after our Tinder match, St. Patty's Day Guy reached out to me to see how I was doing, and he asked if we could meet. I again felt the tug of wanting closure pulling at my insides, so I agreed. When I saw St. Patty's Day Guy, he greeted me as if nothing had happened, but I wasn't going to let him off the hook quite so easily. I initiated a discussion about how things turned bad so suddenly, and we engaged in an uncomfortable adult conversation.

At first, St. Patty's Day Guy said he didn't know why he reacted the way he did, but I could tell that he wasn't being honest. When I suggested that maybe he had started to really care for me and then freaked out when I decided I was moving, he agreed that was an accurate description of how he was feeling. He confessed that he saw a future with me and that he had grown to have deep feelings for me. It's unfortunate that he was never able to communicate that while we were dating.

We resolved to move forward as friends, and we ventured to a few of my favorite bars in the city that night so that I could experience them one more time before I moved in two weeks. We both drank copious amounts of alcohol, which of course means that we made excellent decisions.

Later in the evening, St. Patty's Day Guy started kissing me and alluded to wanting to take me back to his place. I turned him down and told him I was casually seeing someone else but that we had agreed that we were exclusively sleeping with each other. St. Patty's Day Guy was less than thrilled.

Sometime around 2am, a few of St. Patty's Day Guy's friends showed up at the bar, and they were asking us to go to a strip club with them, so I decided to bow out at that point. A girl who I had just met started to pressure me into coming along, saying that based on the way St.

Patty's Day Guy was looking at me, she could tell that he would be bummed if I didn't stick around.

I told her he didn't care if I left, and when she further insisted, I drunkenly declared, "He doesn't care about me, okay?!" I didn't realize that St. Patty's Day Guy was standing behind me. He was clearly offended and hurt that I thought he didn't care about me. I tried to explain the situation, but the alcohol prevented me from adequately expressing myself, and, instead, I semi-dramatically announced I was leaving.

A few minutes after I got in the Uber—which felt like it was spinning—St. Patty's Day Guy started texting me, telling me to turn around and come back. I told him no. He told me to come over to his place, put his "dick in [my] mouth" and "ride his face." I said we could talk in the morning when we were sober, but I wasn't going to engage any more conversation that night.

He did text me the next morning, and we both apologized for our drunken decisions. He asked if he could see me that evening, but I told him I had plans, and I explained that I was saying goodbye to all of my friends before I moved, so my availability would be limited in the next few weeks. I told him that I could probably see him later that week, but he asserted that he had tried enough times and he wasn't going to be my second choice.

I attempted to tell him that wasn't the case, but he wouldn't accept that answer. Instead, he randomly called me out on having a casual partner, and he said that I shouldn't tell people about my "sex pact" because it isn't a "good girl" thing to do. I responded by saying he shouldn't slut shame me just because he's hurt. St. Patty's Day Guy assured me he was not hurt. Doubtful.

I wished him well, and I moved on.

Past Laura would have without a doubt crumbled at that point. I am so proud of myself for not only recognizing that I needed someone more emotionally mature and communicative but that I did not allow the way he handled things to break me as I had done in the past. As you've seen in other chapters, I used to see my worth reflected back like a mirror when a guy didn't treat me with respect or appeared to not want me, even when I didn't particularly like him. In this case, I held onto my own worth from within, even when a guy I actually cared for failed to live up to what I deserved.

I still think that St. Patty's Day Guy is overall a good guy who cared deeply for me. He did reach out to me after I moved, and he texted me after my dad died to make sure I was doing okay. He had the best of intentions, but he just wasn't the right person for me.

Despite that, he was the first guy who prioritized me and put effort into our time together, and for that, I will always be grateful. The way things ended also taught me lessons. I learned how important it is for me to find someone who is not only an effective communicator but who is willing and able to openly discuss emotions, even when they're confusing and uncomfortable. St. Patty's Day Guy simply wasn't able to do that.

By the time St. Patty's Day Guy and I said goodbye, I was more confident in the idea that I would one day find a man who consistently treated me well, and I was less convinced that I *needed* such a man in order to believe I was special. I was on my way to knowing who I was and what I wanted, separate from a romantic partner.

THE FIRST DATE DRESS

CHAPTER EIGHT

Mom's Spaghetti Guy

About a month before I wrote this chapter, I had coffee with Mom's Spaghetti Guy, and I told him there would be a chapter recounting my time with him included in my book. The gist of his response was, "Oh no. What did I do?"

I assured him that he was likely going to be

the only guy in the book who would be happy with his part, and, after the relief that accompanied that knowledge, he helped me brainstorm ideas for this portion of the book. Just by telling you that, I think you can guess that I finally had a healthy dating experience, even if it was short-lived.

Mom's Spaghetti Guy and I matched on Bumble shortly after I stopped talking to St. Patty's Day Guy, and we met up for drinks the following week. After deciding I liked him, I outlined what I was pursuing. I told him I was moving to another state in a little over a month and that I wanted one consistent person to spend time with and have fun with until I left. I was looking for a little casual monogamy. He accepted the position without hesitation.

On our second date, we were having such a good time that I was much more forward than what was typical for me, and after a few hours of drinking wine and listening to music at a rooftop bar, he invited me back to his place.

Now, keep in mind, at this point, with the exception of GoTG, I had never had sex with someone who I hadn't been seeing for at least a few weeks, so I was a little nervous and unsure of myself. Thankfully, I already felt comfortable enough with Mom's Spaghetti Guy that I simply told him how I was feeling, and he was extremely nice and understanding.

In a nutshell, the sex that night was great. All three times. One of the best moments, however, was in between rounds one and two, when he initiated a conversation about what was already good and what could be better. He actually wanted to communicate about sex like an adult, which of course made him even more attractive and made the sex even more enjoyable. That was

---

* One of my friends responded to this story by saying, "Aw, baby's first hookup."

the first time I experienced that type of raw communication.

Afterward, when it was clear we wouldn't be having sex again, I wasn't quite sure what I was supposed to do. I figured I would head home after cuddling for a bit, but a series of questions began floating through the anxious space in my mind. How long do I stay before I leave? What if he's expecting me to spend the night? If so, would it be weird for me to ask to use his shower? Do I put my panties back on, or do I sleep naked? If I sleep over, how long do I hang around in the morning? Do I get to brush my teeth? Should I sleep with my makeup on and risk my skin breaking out or take it off and have him see me without makeup? Can I phone a friend?

Instead of lying in apprehension, I simply said, "I don't know the protocol here, so whenever I'm supposed to leave, just let me know, and I'll go." He laughed a little and said that he thought I would stay over. I pondered the proposition before deciding I would rather sleep in my own bed, and he kindly drove me home, even though I only lived a few blocks from him.

Again, to most people, this would be a normal occurrence, but it was a huge moment for me. Even a few months prior, I wouldn't have wanted to go home. I would have stayed over purely because I had a bad habit of developing an attachment to anyone with whom I was intimate, no matter the level of intimacy or the seriousness of the dating scenario. Leaving Mom's Spaghetti Guy's house that night meant that I was beginning to see myself as a whole person, separate from a man. My worth was not dependent on whether or not he wanted me. It felt liberating.

There was also something freeing for both of

us in knowing that our relationship had an expiration date. We had the space to completely be ourselves because, in the end, I was moving, and we wouldn't be together anyway. There was nothing to lose.

Even better, when we were being our unabridged, undiluted selves, we genuinely liked each other and enjoyed each other's company. It was more than just sex (although we had plenty of that too) but less than a serious relationship. We went on dates, stayed in and watched Netflix together, and spent hours lying in bed just talking. It was somewhat ironic that the guy who was supposed to just be my hookup ended up treating me better than every other man in this book.

Mom's Spaghetti Guy seemed to truly appreciate me for who I was, even pieces of me that others had deemed undesirable. I had been dating people who didn't value some of my favorite things about myself. When I shared with Mom's Spaghetti Guy my experiences with guys who weren't interested in me once I told them I was ambitious in my career,[**] he was taken aback. I recounted multiple first dates that seemed to be going well until I mentioned my doctoral program, and one guy literally said, "Oh... You're getting your Ph.D.? So, you're, like, smart, and want a career?" Instead of saying that with excitement as one would expect, it was presented with hints of disgust.

Mom's Spaghetti Guy couldn't believe that some men still held such antiquated views of women. He was attracted to my ambition and drive instead of repelled by it. He gave me hope that other men would be drawn to me *because* of those qualities and not in spite of them.

Even in the one instance that Mom's

[**] Keep in mind, I'm from the South, and people aren't *always* as progressive there.

Spaghetti Guy wasn't particularly great (because no one is perfect), he handled the situation so well that it was still a positive experience. One night, I initiated a booty call, and Mom's Spaghetti Guy came over after he had been drinking most of the evening. Things started out fine, then, when we switched positions, he had a failure to launch situation.

I tried to stay into it as long as I could, but I was lying on my stomach for a significant amount of time while he attempted to achieve lift off. At a certain point, it was clear that it wasn't going to happen. When I stopped being enthusiastic, Mom's Spaghetti Guy rolled over and said, "You didn't even try."

I sat there in silence for a moment, deciding how to proceed. I could have returned to what I had always done and kept my mouth shut. After all, we were never going to be in a real relationship anyway, so what was the point? Or,

I could have used that as the perfect opportunity to practice expressing my feelings in a healthy, appropriate manner.

I calmly told him that what he said bothered me, especially since I made a solid effort to keep things going, and I asserted that what happened (or didn't happen) had absolutely nothing to do with me.

He immediately apologized and explained that because he was embarrassed he deflected his feelings instead of sitting in the discomfort. We talked about it a little while longer, and I was impressed with how solidly and quickly he owned up to his mistake. He even sent an apology message to me the following morning, despite the fact that we had already resolved the issue. That experience helped me see how conflict should be handled in healthy romantic partnerships.

Of course, I was far from perfection as well.

A few nights later, Mom's Spaghetti Guy and I were lying in bed, and he said something about "mom's spaghetti." I asked what he was referencing. He said he was referring to the song "Lose Yourself," and I laughed as I told him those weren't the correct words. I then proceeded to rap the entire first verse of the song, substituting the "correct" lyrics of, "mom's forgetting he's nervous."

He wavered ever so slightly but still tried to hold true to his belief that he was right, so I Googled the lyrics to prove him wrong. I was so confident that I knew the words that I didn't even glance at the search results before I shoved the phone in his face and said, "See!" He then informed me that, even according to Google, I was indeed wrong.

Although I was a little too cocky, and I'm sure that annoyed him, it wasn't really an issue, and we laughed about it for an absurdly long time. I did genuinely appreciate the fact that he challenged me on it. Because I tend to say things with bursts of confidence, especially when I'm sure that I'm right, not many people question what I say. Mom's Spaghetti Guy showed me that I like being challenged by a man because it pushes me to grow.

The only other "problem" we encountered presented itself during a weekend when a hurricane was due to hit our city. I expressed to Mom's Spaghetti Guy that I was nervous to be living alone during what was supposed to be horrific winds and flooding, and he suggested that we "weather the storm together." In my mind, that meant that we were going to stay together until the storm passed. I think to him, it meant we were going to spend a maximum of 16 hours together.

Mom's Spaghetti Guy came over that Friday afternoon, just before the hurricane was supposed to hit. Because I had sold almost all of my furniture in preparation for my impending move, I no longer owned a couch or a bed, so I decided to build a fort out of blankets, boxes, and pillows for us to cuddle up in while we hunkered down.

We started an episode of the show we had been watching together, and then we had sex in the fort. It looked as if the storm was going to be delayed, so after a few hours together, we decided to walk to his house where his roommates were cooking dinner. Then, I stayed the night.

The next morning, the storm was still taking its sweet time to make landfall, so we found the only open grocery store and bought coffee and food. Mom's Spaghetti Guy cooked me breakfast, and as he pushed eggs around a pan, he started saying things like, "I really just want to watch cartoons all morning" and "I'm really looking forward to a lazy day to do nothing." I definitely did not pick up on the subtle hints that he wanted me to leave.

Halfway through eating my scrambled eggs, and after a few more similar comments, the light bulb went off, and I realized he was hoping I would go home at that point. I was so embarrassed that I overstayed my welcome, but I was also nervous about being alone for the impending storm, so I acted quiet and distant while he drove me home. The "hurricane" ended up just being a light drizzle, making me feel even worse for acting the way I did, so I sent an apology text.

A few days later, we talked about it in person, and everything was fine. Toward the end of our conversation, I said, "Hey, at least I can admit when I'm wrong." To which he replied, "Yeah, but I have to cite 5 sources in APA format just to prove you're wrong."

I was a little taken aback by that comment, and for a split second, I felt hurt that he viewed me as such a difficult know-it-all. Then, in a very freeing moment, I realized that I didn't actually care what he thought of me—not because he was temporary, but because I didn't need his approval or validation. I was done asking permission to be loveable.

I did take something away from his comment though, and I acknowledged that I should probably check myself more often in times like that, but I was able to make that connection without letting his comment impact my self-worth. I could separate his statement from my insecurity.

◆ ◆ ◆

On one of our final evenings together, Mom's Spaghetti Guy took me to his favorite restaurant, and we had the best time talking, laughing, and eating great food. While we were driving back to my place, he brought up that I previously told him I had never had sex in a car, and he asked if I wanted him to park so we could change that. I, of course, said yes. We pulled over on a deserted road, and I felt like a teenager as we clambered into the backseat of his Jeep.

The radio was on, and partway through, the song "Dreams" by The Cranberries filled the speakers, which—FYI—is the perfect song to play in the background during car sex. Just as he was getting close to finishing, however, the song ended, and in its place, we heard Right Said Fred declare, "I'm too sexy for my shirt." I laughed, then felt bad about laughing, *but* because Mom's Spaghetti Guy wasn't a narcissist, everything turned out just fine.

On the ride back to my house, Mom's Spaghetti Guy and I talked about the perfection of "Dreams" in that moment, and then he found the song on Spotify and blared it while we sang/yodeled at the top of our lungs.

A few days later, I stopped by his house to say a final goodbye, and it was hard. I'm not going to lie, somewhere along the way, I caught feelings, and I think he did too.

If I hadn't moved, I don't think we would still be together, because there were a few things that didn't align that probably would have caused issues if we had been in a serious, long-term relationship. But, what we had, in the time we had it, was exactly what I needed. Mom's Spaghetti Guy raised the bar and set the new standard for what I was going to accept in the future, and for that, I am incredibly thankful.

Even though we weren't quite right for each other romantically, I still consider Mom's Spaghetti Guy to be a good friend, and he knows that if he ever needed me, I would be there for him. He is truly a great guy.

The next morning, I drove off towards my new life—a heightened self-worth in tow. As I started my car, I played "Dreams" at full blast, then I drove away and never looked back at what could have been.

THE FIRST DATE DRESS

EPILOGUE

Online dating is a lot like going to the Goodwill outlet. For those of you who haven't experienced this phenomenon, a Goodwill outlet is essentially a warehouse-sized room containing giant dumpter-esque bins filled with a bunch of crap. It's a little overwhelming at first, but it's also exciting not knowing what you might uncover. Will I find a gorgeous dress with pockets, or will the bins be filled with blankets smelling faintly of urine? Anything is possible. You can find some wonderful treasures as long as you're patient enough to sift through the things that don't fit quite right, things you don't find aesthetically pleasing, and things that have questionable histories. So, it's exactly like online dating. Sometimes it feels as if there is a never-ending supply of prospects on dating apps, but—at least for me—it certainly took time to come across someone I actually wanted to date in any significant way.

I'm sure that this final portion of the book would be abundantly more satisfying to you if I told the story of how I fell in love with an amazing man who I'm currently dating—someone who treats me exceptionally well, appreciates me, and inspires me to be a better person every day. I will neither confirm nor deny if that statement is true, because even if it is, that has never been what this book is about.

Regardless of whether or not I found a person with whom I want to share my life, a person who is giving and driven and considerate and affectionate, I am still a whole person worthy of great things. I have finally reached a place in my journey where I feel deserving of love and content in myself without a romantic partner.

It has been amazing to look back at the person I used to be—so fragile and unsure—and to see such powerful growth over a year and a half of self-reflection and self-work. Although at the time, the experiences chronicled in this book were largely negative pieces of my life, I am exceptionally grateful that I had the opportunity to learn so much about myself, even if the revelations came through unfortunate dating scenarios accompanied by corsages, hickeys, and "dead" phones.

I know my self-work isn't over. There are still things I need to address from my past that I notice impacting my emotional state from time to time, but I am consistently striving to not let residual relationship trauma yield any significant power over me. I am no longer allowing men from my past, present, or future to define my worth as a woman. Instead, I am dwelling in a scared space within myself that tells me I am beautiful, interesting, and damn well deserving of real love. I found my "forever person" within myself.

It is both exciting and scary to finally be in a place where I am emotionally ready for a healthy partnership. I spent an absurd amount of time fearing that it wouldn't be possible for me to cultivate a relationship in which I was receiving love with the same ferocity that I gave it. Now I know that my boundless, vast, giving heart will attract someone who feels and loves as endlessly as I do. All I have to do is find him. And maybe I already have.

THE FIRST DATE DRESS

ACKNOWLEDGEMENTS

I want to offer a huge thank you to my editor and dear friend, Callie Milburn, for not only editing my work, but for inspiring the direction of this book. In addition to those major roles, Callie is also an amazing photographer and captured the lovely shots you see of me in this book and on the back cover. *Callie*—thank you for being such a phenomenal, badass woman who is one of the most supportive friends I could have asked for AND also one of the most talented humans I know. This book wouldn't have become a reality without you.

My friends have been the ultimate support system as they helped me through my divorce, listened to my plethora of dating misadventures, and supported me in this crazy endeavor of publishing my first book. Thank you all for your encouragement and love.

My family has always supported me in all of my big dreams, and I am so grateful for them, especially my mom, who has offered me a lifetime of encouragement. I know my dad would have been insanely proud of me for writing a book, and I wish he could be here to share in this moment with me.

Finally, I want to acknowledge every man who has ever treated me well and showed me what it feels like to be a part of a healthy dating experience. Thank you for giving me enough hope to not give up on love entirely.

ABOUT THE AUTHOR

Laura Giroir Smestad is a native of New Orleans currently residing in the Pacific Northwest. Laura received her Master of Arts in Counseling in 2014 and is now practicing as a Licensed Mental Health Counselor in the state of Washington while pursuing a doctoral degree. Laura is passionate about helping people, both in her professional work and personal life. Through her writing, she strives to inspire others—especially women—to find their own worth from within.

THE FIRST DATE DRESS

APPENDIX

The following screenshots show some top-notch dating app openers I've had the pleasure of receiving[1]:

1.

Sep 18, 2019

Hey :)

Good evening!

I am afraid that if I talk to you too much you won't like me. I am neither mentally nor physically healthy 😅

2.

Oct 12, 2018

Hey :)

Hey there 😜

How's your day going?

Delivered

A lot better if you sit on my face

Report

---

[1] Sadly, some of the strangest ones I've received were deleted long ago.

3.

You know how your parents always say they want the best for you? Well they were talking about me 😜

Mon, Aug 13, 2018, 5:52 PM

Haha wow what a line

 Sent

Thu, Aug 16, 2018, 1:15 PM

Hahah well you cant disappoint maw and paw now 👑

4.

Hey we like all the same shit. That's kinda cool

5.

Hey Laura! Happy Monday! Did you know tonight was the Chinese New Year? Strange that I know that 😅

6.

Hey Laura I think you are suffering from a lack of Vitamin Me

7.

A PhD? Is that a playa hater degree? 😩

8.

They sent you a message:

I just relocated back here closer to family. I work close to the city except for a few days a month. How about you? It's nice to make your acquaintance here 😉 🌸 . I like summer because winter can be dreary sometimes. Brrr. Now it's really hot, except the ocassional rain or clouds. Lol. I like your description and feel like we might have some things in common. You and your profile look great! Do you have any plans for the upcoming Autumn season? What's your favorite season, foods or activities?

Made in the USA
Monee, IL
05 March 2020